The Adventures of Rumi & Baruch Bear

For Little and Big People of All Ages

© Copyright 2020 The Adventures of Rumi and Baruch Bear ™ registered by Invictus Holdings LLC.
Published by Redstone Publishing House.
All rights reserved.
No part of this book may be reproduced or used in any manner
without the written permission of the copyright owner except for use of quotations in a book or book review.

For more information visit www.rumiandbixbybear.com

First Hardcover Edition, January 2021.

eBook ISBN: 978-1-7353986-7-9
Hardcover ISBN: 978-1-7353986-4-8
Library of Congress Control Number: 9781735398648

Illustrations by Nasim Jenabi, Vancouver, Canada

For my parents and brothers—my first friends.

This book is meant for

Part I.

Once upon a time in Tehran, Iran,

there lived a girl named Rumi.

She longed to understand the questions of her heart,

and with her imaginary friend, Baruch Bear, at her side,

she looked for answers.

One day, Iran was no longer safe for Rumi and her family.

Rumi fled Iran and moved to New York with her mother,

grandparents, and great-grandfather.

Rumi liked learning, but on the morning of her first day of Yeshiva,

Rumi cried to Mother, "*Maman*, I do not want to go to Yeshiva school."

Mother became upset, "Why not? Yeshiva and learning Torah are important!"

Grandfather became concerned at Mother's tone. He whispered to her,

"Raise your words, not your voice. It is rain that grows flowers, not thunder."

Grandfather looked lovingly at Mother and continued,

"How do you think the rose ever opened its heart and gave the world all of its beauty?

It felt the encouragement of the sun's light against its being."

As Mother thought about Grandfather's words,

she helped Rumi get ready for Yeshiva.

When they arrived at Yeshiva, Mother asked Rumi what was wrong, but this time gently.

"I stutter, I have an accent, and I am afraid

that n-n-nobody at Yeshiva will understand me," Rumi confessed.

Mother hugged Rumi and kissed her forehead and said:

"*Jooni* dear, I am sorry I raised my voice before.

But remember that when you are afraid, uncertain, or sad,

my love for you is like an endless ocean. It has no beginning and no end."

Mother continued, "Each one of us in our life must acquire for themselves

a teacher and a friend. Yeshiva is the best place to do both."

"But I won't find any friends there," Rumi said sadly.

"Ever since the dawn of your life, friendship heard your name

and it has been running through the schoolyard trying to catch you. You must let it."

Rumi smiled because she knew her mother was right.

Friendship was waiting for her.

At Yeshiva, Rumi saw many new faces.

Rumi gathered all her courage and went to her Rabbi and teacher

to ask him the questions that had been weighing on her heart.

"Can you tell me about friendship?" Rumi asked.

Rabbi looked at Rumi and said, "I cannot tell you much about friendship, but this I do know:

Our sages tell us three things should a person prize: a home, a friend, and a book.

I have learned much from my teachers and from books,

but from my friends, I have learned the most."

Rumi liked what Rabbi said but she wasn't satisfied.

She still wanted to learn more about friendship.

After Yeshiva, Rumi arrived home—sad that she had not made any friends that day at school.

Rumi then prepared for Shabbat,

and later at Shabbat dinner, with her many cousins, she ate lots of *gondi* balls.

Rumi still had many questions on her mind.

"Grandpa-*joon*, Grandma-*joon*, can you tell me about friendship?" Rumi asked.

"Friendship is the water of life! Say *L'Chaim*—to life!" said Grandfather.

And the whole family responded, *"L'Chaim!"*

"My precious Rumi-*joon*," Grandmother continued while smiling at Grandfather,

"Friendship is an act of imagination.

Friendship is looking at the thorn and seeing the rose,

looking at the night and seeing the day."

"What does that mean?" Rumi asked. "I do not understand."

Grandfather explained, "Be patient with the questions of your heart."

Great-grandfather added, "Everything has its time and every type of friendship has its season.

Just as the moon needs time to become full, so does the human heart."

After Shabbat dinner, Rumi sat with Baruch Bear in her bedroom

and wondered about the future.

"What will my life be like when I grow up? Will I have a lot of friends?"

Rumi asked Baruch, her eyes bright with curiosity.

"I do not know the answers," Baruch Bear replied.

"All I can say is this: Who is wise? She who learns from others.

But do not blindly follow the stories of others that came before you.

You must create your own path."

"But I do not want to walk the path alone!" Rumi said anxiously.

"Others may walk the journey *with* you, but nobody can walk it *for* you," said Baruch Bear.

"Can you walk it *with* me, Baruch?" asked Rumi.

"Of course, Rumi! My name means *blessing*. As your inner voice, I will be a *bracha*

— a blessing for you wherever you go," Baruch Bear replied.

"That makes me feel better." Rumi smiled as she yawned.

"*Layla Tob* and *Shab Bekheir*, Baruch Bear."

"Good night, Rumi. Sweet dreams."

Part II.

That night, Rumi had a dream.

She imagined that she and Baruch Bear walked on the great long road called *Life*.

They traveled far and wide.

Rumi looked to her right and to her left,

upwards and downwards,

above the heavens and below the earth,

looking for the answers to all the questions in her heart.

Sometimes Rumi worried if she was walking the correct path,

but Baruch Bear comforted her by saying, "Be patient with your questions.

As you begin to walk the way, the way will appear.

The one who is a seeker, *Hashem*, our God, will always make a finder."

In her dream, Rumi met different kinds of people and tried to be their friend.

Rumi found that friendships could be hard work;

and that some people did not want to be her friend.

Rumi telephoned her grandfather to ask him more about friendship.

Grandfather said, "How beautiful it is to sit amongst friends—*yachad*—which means together.

Two friends are better than one. For if one falls, then the other one can lift up her fellow!

But if you are looking for a friend who is faultless, then you will be friendless.

And if you are annoyed by their every rub, then how will you ever be polished?"

"But Grandpa-*joon*, how do I become polished?" Rumi asked.

"Keep walking the great long road," Grandfather responded.

Thinking about what her grandfather told her, Rumi kept walking the great long road.

Until one day, Baruch Bear asked Rumi:

"You are on this great adventure inside your dreams,

You look to your right and to your left,

upwards and downwards,

above the heavens and below the earth,

looking for the answers to the questions of your heart.

But when will you really begin the journey into yourself?"

"The journey into *myself?* What does that have to do with friendship?" Rumi asked.

"You are the most important person you will ever get to know.

We rarely hear our inner music when we are with others,

but we are still dancing to it," Baruch Bear replied.

There were times along her journey, however, that Rumi felt discouraged.

Rumi wished that she had stayed in the comfort of her home,

that she had never looked to the right and to the left,

upwards and downwards,

above the heavens and below the earth.

"Sometimes the journey is hard," Rumi said to Baruch Bear.

Baruch nodded, "It's okay to feel sad at times.

Brighter days do not always come to you, sometimes you must go to them.

In a night full of darkness, be like the sun who volunteers its light

by doing *hesed*, kindness, to others."

Rumi didn't understand Baruch Bear's words.

But Rumi had *emunah*, faith, that she would find the answers.

As they passed a mountain, Baruch Bear said softly to Rumi,

"Listen. Just learn to listen." "But Baruch!" Rumi exclaimed.

"Rumi! Shhh! There is a voice that does not use words.

Can you hear the trees? Look at the sunset!"

Rumi, with new eyes, saw the world and all of its beauty.

She turned to the heavens and said, "Blessed is *Hashem*, our God, Lord of the universe,

who forms the wonders of Creation."

She then turned to Baruch Bear and smiled, "Isn't it amazing?"

"What is?" Baruch Bear asked.

"Even after all this time, the sun never says to the earth, '*You owe me.*'

Look what happens with a friendship like that.

It becomes a love that lights the whole sky!" Rumi replied.

Part III.

On *Motzaei Shabbat*, after the sabbath, Rumi had a new dream,

Rumi slowly began to understand friendship.

Rumi looked to her right and to her left,

upwards and downwards,

above the heavens,

and below the earth.

But this time she also looked inwards,

discovering that her inner voice was powerful all on its own.

Rumi continued to travel throughout the world, sharing her inner music with others.

She experienced great new joy in her adventures.

She practiced yoga on the Great Wall of China . . .

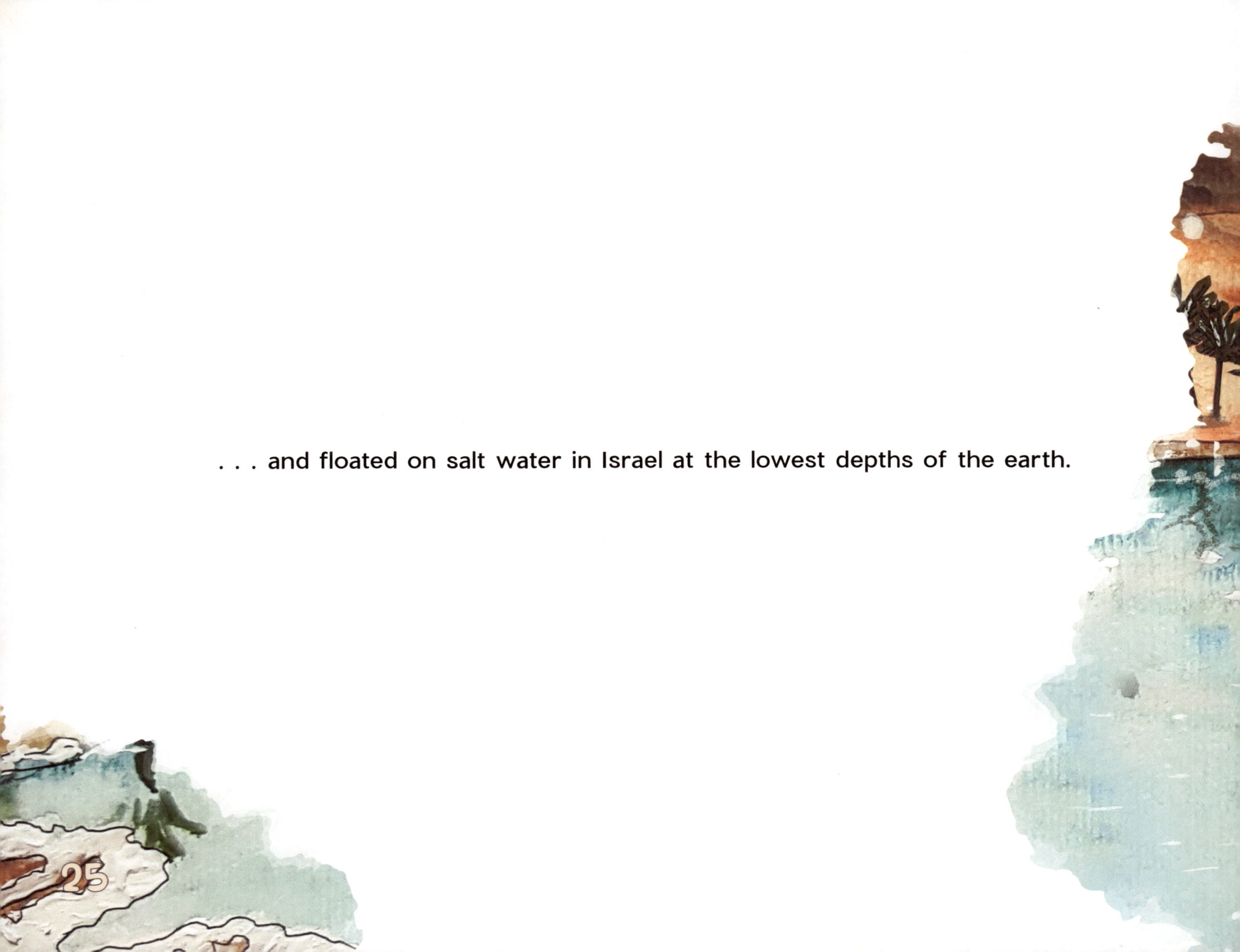

. . . and floated on salt water in Israel at the lowest depths of the earth.

When Rumi's heart was ready, filled with love of itself, she said goodbye to Baruch Bear.

As Baruch Bear departed, he asked Rumi to remember all that they had been through together.

No matter the challenges, stutters, or pain that Rumi experienced along her adventure,

she would always carry Baruch Bear in her heart.

Rumi, alone with her inner voice, kept searching for answers,

grateful for all the questions that *Hashem* gave her.

Rumi never gave up.

Rumi kept going,

and going,

and going.

After Shabbat, Rumi awoke from her dream and, on that Monday, rushed to Yeshiva.

When she arrived, Rumi's classmates were drawn to her strength, confidence, and wisdom.

The kind that forms when someone builds a friendship with themselves.

Rumi had found patience towards the questions of her heart.

From Baruch Bear, she had learned to love the questions themselves,

as if they were stories hidden in secret rooms, waiting to be discovered.

"Will you give us the answers to our questions?" Rumi's new friends asked.

"Do not seek the answers from me, for I cannot give them to you," Rumi responded.

"Because then, you would not be able to *live* your own questions."

"How do we live our questions?" they all asked Rumi.

"L-L-Live the questions in the now. Ask *Hashem* for help.

Then one day, maybe without even knowing it,

your heart will live its w-w-way into the answers."

With her family, friends, and *Hashem* at her side,

Rumi explored to the right and to the left,

upwards and downwards,

above the heavens and below the earth.

They looked inwards.

They inspired each other;

and they inspired others.

They befriended others;

they tried to never say gossip and bad words, *La-showne Ha-rah*, about others.

And together they lived out the questions of the human heart.

Additional Information

Please visit www.rumiandbixbybear.com to learn more about the poet Rumi.
On the website, readers can also download a free parent and teacher guidebook
designed to facilitate discussions among children and parents, teachers and students.

CPSIA information can be obtained
at www.ICGtesting.com
Printed in the USA
BVHW090214250422
635162BV00017B/28